· RICK CAMPBELL ·

GENERAL
KNOWLEDGE
TRIVIA
QUIZ
BOOK

· TRIVIAL TRUTHS ·

*The author wishes to thank all those
who provided questions, expertise, and/or encouragement:
Billy MacKay, Mark Lundquist, Sharon Bosley, Scott
Amenn, Sui Mon Wu, Stuart Miller, Tommy Jenkins,
Carol Kelly-Gangi, Claire Glick, and Hunter Hauk.*

ISBN 0-7607-2106-8

Book design by Lundquist Design, New York

Printed and bound in the United States of America

01 02 03 MP 9 8 7 6 5 4 3 2

OPM

Q: What is the highest mountain in the world?

Q: What is the highest point in North America?

Q: What is the highest point in the 48 contiguous
    United States?

Q: What is the lowest point on land in North America?

Q: What is the lowest point on land in the world?

A: Mt. Everest, in Nepal and Tibet, is 29,028 feet above sea level. The five highest mountains in the world are all in the Himalayas.

A: At 20,320 feet, Mt. McKinley in Alaska is the highest mountain on the continent. The peak is also known by the Athabascan name Denali.

A: The summit of Mt. Whitney in California is 14,494 feet above sea level.

A: Death Valley, also in California, bottoms out at 282 feet below sea level.

A: Earth's lowest point on land is the Dead Sea, in Israel and Jordan, which is 1,312 feet below sea level.

Q: What American-born man became Prime Minister and President of Ireland?

Q: What American became Prime Minister of Israel?

Q: How did Douglas "Wrong Way" Corrigan get his nickname?

Q: Where is Judge Crater?

A: Eamon de Valera, born in New York in 1882, became the Prime Minister, and later President, of the Republic of Ireland.

A: Golda Meir, born in Russia in 1898, grew up in Milwaukee after her family moved there in 1906. She was Prime Minister of Israel from 1969 to 1974.

A: On July 17, 1938, Douglas Corrigan filed a flight plan at Floyd Bennett Field in New York to fly to California, but ended up in Dublin 29 hours later.

A: No one knows.
On August 6, 1930, New York Supreme Court Justice Joseph F. Crater disappeared. After telling friends that he was attending a Broadway play that evening, he removed papers from his files and cashed a check for a large sum. Late that afternoon, he was seen entering a taxi, but hasn't been sighted since.
For decades, people have theorized about the cause of his disappearance: Was he involved in illegal activities? Was he murdered by the underworld? Did he run away? Although Judge Crater was declared officially dead in July 1937, we can still only speculate about why he vanished.

Q: In the sequence "2, 3, 5, 7, 11, 13," what is the next number?

Q: What is litmus paper? What do the colors indicate?

Q: What are the colors of the visible spectrum of light?

Q: What are quasars?

A: 17. These are, in ascending order, the lowest prime numbers. Prime numbers are numbers that cannot be divided by any number other than themselves and the number one.

A: Litmus paper is paper treated with a dye that measures the acidity and alkalinity of a solution, or its pH. If the paper turns red, it is acidic; if it turns blue, it is alkaline.

A: Red, orange, yellow, green, blue, indigo, violet, which science students sometimes remember as "Roy G. Biv." Beyond the visible spectrum of light are ultraviolet, which is used in black lights and x-rays, and infrared, the most important use being remote controls for televisions.

A: Although scientific debates still rage about the nature of quasars, they appear to be stars that are moving away from earth at great speeds, as shown by the red shifts in their spectra. They may also be distant galaxies.

Q: The Quarrymen included the nucleus of what well-known rock band?

Q: What were The Who called before they were The Who?

Q: Which member of the Grateful Dead inspired an ice cream flavor?

Q: What is the name of the only Broadway show tune recorded by the Beatles?

Q: What recording company released the first recordings of Elvis Presley?

A: John Lennon, Paul McCartney, and George Harrison were all members of The Quarrymen. Ringo Starr joined much later, after they had become the Beatles.

A: The High Numbers, who released one record, "I'm the Face."

A: Cherry Garcia is a flavor of Ben and Jerry's ice cream (and frozen yogurt) named after the lead singer of the Grateful Dead, the late Jerry Garcia.

A: "'Til There Was You," from Meredith Wilson's *The Music Man.*

A: Sun Records, Sam Phillips's little Memphis music company, pressed the first Elvis Presley records in 1954. "That's All Right, Mama" was on the hit side.

Q: What was known as Seward's Folly? When did it occur?

Q: In what year did Alaska become a state?

Q: When was the Louisiana Purchase?

Q: When did Lewis and Clark embark on their famous expedition to explore this new American land?

Q: What is the continental divide, and where is it?

A: When the United States bought Alaska from Russia in 1867, the American press lambasted Secretary of State William Seward, who negotiated the deal, for the "outrageous" $7,200,000 purchase price.

A: Alaska became the 49th state of the Union in 1959.

A: In 1803, Napoleon sold 800,000 square miles of the Louisiana Territory to the United States for $11.25 million. The purchase doubled the size of the nation.

A: On May 14, 1804, Meriwether Lewis and William Clark left St. Louis to begin a transcontinental exploratory mission for President Thomas Jefferson. Their cross-country expedition took two and a half years.

A: The continental divide is the drainage divide separating rivers flowing toward the opposite sides of a continent. In the United States, the Continental Divide follows the crest of the Rocky Mountains. West of the divide, the waters empty into the Pacific; east of the divide, river waters eventually flow into the Atlantic, sometimes via Hudson Bay or the Gulf of Mexico.

Q: What is the literary significance of June 16, 1904?

Q: Ernest Hemingway asserted that all modern American literature comes from one book. What novel was Hemingway praising?

Q: "That's not writing; it's typing" was one American author's comment on another's work. Who was talking about whom?

Q: One famous American poet was a West Point cadet. Who was he and how did he fare?

A: It's Bloomsday, the day in which all of the events occur in James Joyce's novel *Ulysses*.

A: Mark Twain's *The Adventures of Huckleberry Finn*.

A: Truman Capote on Jack Kerouac.

A: Edgar Allan Poe's brief stint at the U.S. Military Academy brought mixed results. After less than eight months there, he was court-martialed and dismissed from the Academy in January 1831. However, before he left, Poe convinced more than 130 of his classmates to subsidize the publication of his second book of poetry.

Q: Which president of the Confederate States of America was a West Point graduate?

Q: Where did the Commanding General of the Confederate forces surrender to the Commanding General of the Union forces?

Q: How did Confederate General "Stonewall" Jackson earn his nickname?

Q: Which Civil War general popularized a new men's hairstyle, which became known as "sideburns"?

A: Jefferson Davis, the only President of the Confederacy, graduated from the United States Military Academy in 1828.

A: On April 9, 1865, Confederate General Robert E. Lee surrendered to U.S. General Ulysses S. Grant at the Appomattox Courthouse, in Virginia. Both were West Point graduates.

A: General Thomas Jonathan Jackson, also a West Point graduate, earned his nickname at the First Battle of Bull Run (1861), by holding his ground.

A: Union General Ambrose E. Burnside earned a niche in history for his mutton chops, which became known as "sideburns." He, too, graduated from West Point.

Q: What is the largest lake in the world?

Q: Which lake is the largest in North America?

Q: List the Great Lakes in order of size, based on surface area.

Q: Which Great Lake is the deepest?

Q: Which of the Great Lakes does not border on Canada?

A: The Caspian Sea, with a surface area of 143,244 square miles. This salty lake borders Azerbaijan, Russia, Kazakhstan, Turkmenistan, and Iran.

A: Lake Superior, the largest lake in North America, and the second-largest lake in the world, has a surface area of 31,700 square miles.

A: From largest to smallest: Lakes Superior, Huron, Michigan, Erie, and Ontario.

A: The deepest of the five Great Lakes is Lake Superior. Its lowest point is 1,332 feet deep, almost enough to submerge the Sears Tower.

A: Lake Michigan is wholly in the United States, bordering on Illinois, Wisconsin, Michigan, and Indiana.

Q: Who was the first woman elected to the U.S. House of Representatives?

Q: When did women get the right to vote in national elections?

Q: Where was the first women's rights convention held?

Q: What was the first co-educational college in the United States?

Q: Who was the first woman sworn in as a Supreme Court Justice?

A: Jeanette Rankin, Republican from Montana, was the first woman elected to the House of Representatives in 1916.

A: The ratification of the nineteenth amendment on August 18, 1920, guaranteed women access to the ballot box.

A: Organized by Elizabeth Cady Stanton, the first Women's Rights Convention convened on July 19, 1848, in Seneca Falls, New York. A "Declaration of Sentiments and Resolutions" was issued at the convention.

A: Opened in 1833, Oberlin College admitted both men and women as students.

A: Sandra Day O'Connor took the oath in 1981.

Q: How many tentacles does an octopus have? How many tentacles does a squid have?

Q: How many legs does a spider have? How many eyes?

Q: Why do spiders never get caught in their webs?

Q: How fast can dragonflies fly?

Q: Why do fireflies flash?

A: The octopus has eight tentacles. The squid has ten, two of which are specialized. The squid is no wimp—the giant squid is the largest creature on earth without a backbone, sometimes growing to 55 feet long and weighing 2.5 tons.

A: All spiders have eight legs. Most spiders have eight eyes, but some also have six. There are spiders with two, four, and even twelve eyes.

A: Spiders can get caught in webs, but it very rarely happens. The tips of their legs are especially built, and the oil on their legs keeps them free-footed.

A: They can achieve speeds of up to 30 miles per hour.

A: A chemical reaction related to the mating process causes the bursts of light. The male and female fireflies have different patterns of flashing, but it is much too complicated to discuss here.

Q: What educational first did W. E. B. DuBois attain?

Q: What did Rosa Parks do on December 1, 1955?

Q: When did Jackie Robinson become the first black baseball player in the modern major leagues?

Q: Who was the first black Supreme Court justice?

Q: Who was the first African American to win the Nobel Peace Prize?

A: When he received his doctorate in 1895, W. E. B. DuBois became the first African American to receive a Ph.D. from Harvard.

A: On December 1, 1955, she refused to give up her seat on a bus in Montgomery, Alabama. This act of bravery led to a boycott of Montgomery businesses, and was a major step in the battle for civil rights in the United States.

A: Jackie Robinson, already a star in the Negro Leagues, joined the Brooklyn Dodgers in 1947.

A: Thurgood Marshall was appointed by President Lyndon B. Johnson to the U.S. Supreme Court in 1967.

A: Fourteen years before Martin Luther King Jr. won the honor, African-American Ralph Bunche received the Nobel Peace Prize in 1950. Bunche earned the honor for his work as a mediator in Palestine while serving as the director of the United Nations Division of Trusteeship.

Q: Who invented the Spinning Jenny? What is it?

Q: Match the inventors with the inventions.

Carrier	Machine gun
Babbage	Mercury thermometer
Nesmith	Air conditioning
Birdseye	Correction fluid
Gatling	Frozen food (commercial)
Fahrenheit	Calculating machine

Q: When was the zipper invented?

A: In 1764, Englishman James Hargreaves invented a hand-powered machine, which, by adding spindles to the spinning wheel, was able to spin numerous threads simultaneously. This increased yarn production many times over. He named the machine for his daughter, Jenny.

A: Carrier = Air conditioning
Babbage = Calculating machine
Nesmith = Correction fluid
Birdseye = Frozen food
Gatling = Machine gun
Fahrenheit = Mercury thermometer

A: Whitcomb Judson, an engineer from Chicago, patented the first zipper in 1893 and exhibited it at the Chicago World's Fair. However, the new invention didn't catch on (so to speak) until B. F. Goodrich put zippers in his new product—rubber galoshes. Goodrich also coined the term. Until then, zippers were called "hookless fasteners."

Q: What was the name of the Ewings' ranch on the TV show *Dallas*?

Q: Which actors played the following TV doctors: Dr. Kildare? Ben Casey? Dr. Welby on *Marcus Welby, M.D.*? Dr. Ross on *E.R.*?

Q: Warren Beatty appeared as a regular in what popular fifties sitcom?

Q: Every Tuesday, *The Honeymooners'* Ralph Kramden plays pool; every Thursday, he bowls. What does Ralphie Boy do on Friday nights?

Q: Who was the narrator on the 1950s television series *The Untouchables*?

A: South Fork.

A: They were played, respectively, by Richard Chamberlain, Vince Edwards, Robert Young, and George Clooney. Mark Jenkins also played Dr. Kildare on the short-lived 1972 series *Young Dr. Kildare*.

A: In the 1959-1960 season of *The Many Loves of Dobie Gillis*, Beatty played Milton Armitage, Dobie's rich rival for the affections of Thalia Menninger (played by Tuesday Weld).

A: He spends every Friday night down at the Raccoon Lodge.

A: Newspaperman and gossip columnist Walter Winchell received $25,000 to narrate each episode of this weekly drama. On this partially fact-based show, machine gun-wielding gangbuster Eliot Ness (portrayed by Robert Stack) tracked down assorted real-life mobsters, such as Frank Nitti (played by Bruce Gordon). The show, which aired from 1959 to 1963, was among the most violent—and popular—shows of its time.

Q: Where are the Weddell and Ross Seas?

Q: Who was the first person to reach the South Pole?

Q: Who was the first person to fly over the South Pole?

Q: What percentage of the world's fresh water is in the frozen ice mass of Antarctica?

Q: Which nation owns Antarctica?

A: Antarctica.

A: The Norwegian explorer Roald Amundsen, on December 13, 1911.

A: In November 1929, American Admiral Richard E. Byrd flew his tri-motor plane, the *Floyd Bennett*, across the South Pole. Byrd named the plane for his pilot from several earlier explorations.

A: 70%.

A: None. It has been declared an area for scientific study.

Q: One team won eight consecutive National Basketball Association championships. What team? Which years?

Q: What player averaged 50 points for a complete NBA season?

Q: How many seasons did the American Basketball Association survive?

Q: Who holds the record for most lifetime points in the NBA?

Q: What team has won the most NCAA championships in men's basketball?

A: The Boston Celtics won NBA titles every year from 1959 through 1966.

A: Wilt Chamberlain. During the 1961-1962 NBA season, the Philadelphia center averaged 50.4 points per game. On March 2, 1962, he scored 100 points in a game against New York.

A: Nine seasons; from 1967 to 1976. After the league ceased operations, four ABA teams joined the National Basketball Association: Indiana, Denver, San Antonio, and the New York Nets.

A: During his career, Kareem Abdul Jabbar scored 38,387 points. Michael Jordan has the highest career scoring average with 31.5 points point per game.

A: UCLA has won eleven NCAA championships. The University of Kentucky is second, having won the crown seven times.

Q: In what year was gold first discovered in California's Sutter's Mill?

Q: When did Mrs. O'Leary's cow cause the Chicago fire?

Q: When did the great San Francisco earthquake strike?

Q: Name the date and the day of the week of the Stock Market Crash of 1929.

A: 1848. On January 24th of that year, James Marshall
    panned the first gold nuggets there. By 1849, 80,000
    prospectors had arrived in the territory. Within a few
    years, more than 500,000 people had migrated to
    California.

A: Much of Chicago was destroyed by fire on October 8-11,
    1871, but to this day, it is unclear how it started. Mrs.
    O'Leary's bovine became the fall guy (cow).

A: On April 18, 1906, San Francisco suffered its worst seis-
    mic upheaval. This quake and the fires and aftershocks
    that followed left 503 dead and caused $350 million in
    damages.

A: The 1929 disaster took several days to unfold, but most
    believe the date of the actual crash to be October 29th,
    now known as "Black Tuesday." The panic had actually
    started on the previous Thursday, October 24th.

Q: Before they became famous singers, James Brown, Dean Martin, and Jackie Wilson all participated in what sport?

Q: Who were the songwriters for many of Jackie Wilson's early records, including his first hit, "Reet Petite"?

Q: Where was the original recording studio for Motown Records?

Q: What was the title of the first hit record by James Brown and the Famous Flames?

Q: What was the name of Dean Martin's partner in a popular song and comedy act?

A: In their youth, all three were amateur boxers. Jackie
    Wilson was even a Golden Gloves Champion in Detroit.
    Dean Martin boxed under the name of Kid Crochet.

A: Berry Gordy Jr. and Tyron Carlo. Gordy went on to found
    Motown Records.

A: Hitsville USA was the name given to the studios at 2648
    West Grand Boulevard in Detroit, where many of the first
    Motown hits were recorded.

A: "Please, Please, Please," originally released on Federal
    Records in 1956, was not only their first hit, it was their
    first record.

A: Dean Martin and Jerry Lewis were a popular team in the
    1950s, making many movie, television, and radio appear-
    ances together.

Q: What is the longest river in the world?

Q: What is the largest lake in Africa?

Q: What is the longest river in the United States?

Q: List the world's oceans in order of size.

Q: Is it possible to drown in the Dead Sea?

A: The longest is the Nile in Africa, which flows 4,160 miles
     to the Mediterranean Sea. The next two rivers in length
     are the Amazon and the Chang Jiang (Yangtze) Rivers.

A: Lake Victoria, one of the sources of the Nile, is the largest
     lake on the continent. Its 28,820 square miles make it the
     third-largest lake in the world.

A: There are two possible answers: The Mississippi River,
     which flows 2,340 miles from Lake Itasca, Minnesota, to
     the Gulf of Mexico, is the longest river in the U.S.; or the
     Mississippi-Missouri-Red Rock River system, which runs
     3,710 miles from Montana to the Gulf of Mexico.

A: From the largest to the smallest: The Pacific, Atlantic,
     Indian, and Arctic Oceans.

A: Yes, but not very easily. The high salt content of the Dead
     Sea causes one to float effortlessly.

Q: How did Jesse James die?

Q: Who fought at the OK Corral on October 26, 1881?

Q: What was Annie Oakley's real name?

Q: What hand in poker is known as a "dead man's hand"?

A: There are various theories about Jesse James's death, but the generally accepted one is that on April 3, 1882, while he was straightening a picture on a wall, James was shot in the back of the head by Robert Ford. Thereafter, Ford was known as "the dirty coward who shot Mr. Howard"; Howard being Jesse James's last known alias.

A: As every cowboy movie-goer knows, the Earp Brothers and Doc Holliday exchanged gunfire with the outlaw Clanton Gang and the McLaury brothers. For added fire-power, Virgil Earp, the sheriff of Tombstone, Arizona, had deputized his brothers, Wyatt and Morgan.

A: Phoebe Anne Moses. Although she never lived further west than Ohio, Annie Oakley won well-deserved fame as an expert rifle and shotgun marksman in Buffalo Bill's Wild West Show.

A: On August 2, 1876, Wild Bill Hickok was shot in the back of the head by Jack McCall in a saloon in Deadwood, South Dakota. Hickok died holding a pair of aces and a pair of eights, which became known as a "dead man's hand."

Q: When was the first Woolworth's store opened?

Q: When did Sears, Roebuck and Co. begin business?

Q: Where did J.C. Penney originate?

Q: Barnes & Noble was founded in what year?

A: Frank W. Woolworth opened the first five-and-dime store in Utica, New York, on February 22, 1879, but soon after its opening the store failed. Only after opening another store in Lancaster, Pennsylvania, in June 1879 did Woolworth meet success with his chain. The last Woolworth's store closed in 1997.

A: A year after starting in Minneapolis in 1886, the R.W. Sears Watch Company moved to Chicago, where they hired a Mr. Roebuck as a watchmaker. In 1893, Sears, Roebuck and Co. was formed and began to issue the first of its famous catalogues.

A: In 1902, James Cash Penney opened his first store in Kemmerer, Wyoming.

A: In 1873, Mr. Barnes and Mr. Noble formed a bookselling organization in Wheaton, Illinois. The company moved to New York a few years later.

Q: What country has the largest population?

Q: What country has the smallest population?

Q: In what country do people speak the language Esperanto?

Q: What do Istanbul, Constantinople, and Byzantium have in common?

A: China has the world's largest population: An estimated 1.2 billion people. India has the second largest population with over 940 million people.

A: The one-half square mile Vatican city-state, with 1,000 residents.

A: Nowhere. It is an artificial international language, which never became accepted.

A: They are three historical names for the same city, present-day Istanbul, capital of Turkey.

Q: What historic event occurred on July 14, 1789?

Q: What happened on June 28, 1914?

Q: When did World War II begin?

Q: When was the Berlin Wall built? When did it come down?

Q: How many people died in the flu epidemic of 1918-1919?

A: On that day, an angry French crowd stormed Paris's Bastille Prison. July 14th is now commemorated in France as Bastille Day.

A: On June 28, 1914, a Serbian activist assassinated Archduke Francis Ferdinand, the heir to the throne of Austria-Hungary, and his wife, in Sarajevo. Within two months, tensions had escalated into the First World War.

A: The actual fighting began when German troops crossed the border into Poland on September 1, 1939. Pledged to support Poland, Britain and France declared war on Germany two days later. The United States did not enter the war until December 1941.

A: The Berlin Wall was constructed in August 1961 to stop escapes by East Germans to West Berlin. The wall was dismantled in 1989.

A: In the three waves of the 1918-1919 flu epidemic, at least twenty million people succumbed. Indeed, many estimates run as high as thirty million dead. Coming on the heels of the First World War (in which *only* ten million perished), the pandemic spread more quickly and widely because of the large troop movements of the time.

Q: Who was the only heavyweight boxing champion to end his career undefeated?

Q: When did Joe Louis first become the heavyweight champion?

Q: Who was nicknamed the "Manassa Mauler"?

Q: What fight was called "The Thrilla in Manila"?

A: When he retired from boxing in 1956, heavyweight champion Rocky Marciano had a professional record of 49 victories and no defeats or draws. He had held the world championship for four years.

A: On June 22, 1937, Joe Louis, also known as "The Brown Bomber," knocked out James J. Braddock, thus beginning a twelve-year reign as the world heavyweight champion.

A: Born in Manassa, Colorado, former barroom bouncer Jack Dempsey.

A: The aptly named Muhammad Ali-Joe Frazier championship fight in 1975. Ali won the hard-fought match when Frazier was unable to come out for the 15th round.

Q: What year was the Magna Carta signed?

Q: Who fought in the Hundred Years War? (Did it really last a hundred years?)

Q: When did Marco Polo go to China?

Q: What are the names of the wives of Henry VIII?

A: King John of England signed the Magna Carta in 1215. It guaranteed the privileges of nobles and church against the monarchy, and also assured the right to a jury trial.

A: France and England were officially at war from 1334 to 1453, but during much of that time they fought few battles. It was not until 1565 that the English were forced out of Calais, their last foothold on the French mainland.

A: In 1260, Marco Polo, son of a Venetian merchant and explorer, accompanied his father on an overland journey to China. His record of his Asian adventures, written while he was imprisoned, became the most famous travel book in history.

A: Henry VIII, who ruled England from 1509 to 1547, married six times. His not-always-so-lucky wives were as follows: Catherine of Aragon, whom he divorced; Anne Boleyn, whom he beheaded; Jane Seymour, who died during childbirth; Anne of Cleves, divorced; Catherine Howard, another decapitation; and Catherine Parr, who, somehow, outlived him.

Q: How many of the original Allman Brothers were actually brothers?

Q: How are the Beach Boys related?

Q: What was the relationship between Gladys Knight and the Pips?

Q: How are the Bee Gees related?

Q: Where did the Doobie Brothers get their name?

A: Two: Duane and Gregg.

A: Three of the original Beach Boys were brothers—Brian, Carl, and Dennis Wilson. One, Mike Love, was a cousin, and the other, Al Jardine, was a neighbor.

A: Gladys's back-up singers, the Pips, consisted of two of her cousins, and her brother, Merald ("Bubba").

A: Robin, Barry, and Maurice Gibb are brothers.

A: A "doobie" is slang for a marijuana cigarette. They are not actually blood relations.

Q: When was "The Star-Spangled Banner" written?
What inspired Francis Scott Key to write "The
Star-Spangled Banner"?

Q: What is the Monroe Doctrine?

Q: What happened at the Alamo?

Q: When did the Erie Canal open?

A: Francis Scott Key wrote the American national anthem after watching the unsuccessful bombardment of Baltimore's Fort McHenry by British ships on the night of September 14, 1814.

A: In 1823, President James Monroe declared that the Americas were to be free from colonialism and interference from Europe.

A: Under siege by thousands of Mexican soldiers led by dictator Santa Ana, the 189 defenders of the Texas Republic at the Alamo held out for 13 days to the last man—from February 23 to March 6, 1836. Among the illustrious defenders were William Travis, Davy Crockett, and Jim Bowie.

A: The first boat left Buffalo on October 26, 1825, and arrived in New York City on November 4th. By connecting Lake Erie to the Hudson River, the Erie Canal radically decreased the shipping time between cities in the interior and the Atlantic coast.

Q: Where was the game of golf invented?

Q: Who has won more Masters tournaments than any other golfer?

Q: When did Tiger Woods win the Masters tournament for the first time?

Q: Which of the following athletes is not a member of the Professional Bowlers Association Hall of Fame?

Dave Ferraro   Chris Antley

Carmen Salvino   Don Carter

Roy Buckley

A: Scotland is considered the birthplace of the sport, golf having flourished there since the 15th century. Even then, an exerting round was followed by a refreshing trip to the local tavern.

A: Jack Nicklaus, with six Masters victories.

A: On April 13, 1997, Tiger Woods won his first Masters tournament at Augusta National Golf Course. He became the first person of color to gain that coveted title.

A: Chris Antley is a Kentucky Derby-winning jockey, not a professional bowler.

Q: Which state has the largest population?

Q: Which state has the smallest population?

Q: What is the world's busiest airport?

Q: What is the largest port in the United States in terms of tonnage handled?

Q: What is the southernmost state in the United States?

A: California, with approximately 33 million people.

A: Wyoming, with less than half a million people.

A: Chicago's O'Hare International Airport, which has over 65 million passengers annually.

A: Ranked by tonnage handled, the Port of South Louisiana is America's busiest port, handling 200 million tons of cargo each year.

A: Hawaii, which is located as far south as 18°55' North—at Ka Lae, on the big island of Hawaii. Key West, Florida, is the southernmost point in the forty-eight contiguous states, with a latitude of 24°33' North.

Q: Who was the first elected President of Russia?

Q: What was the name of the dynasty that ruled Russia from 1613 to 1917?

Q: Who was Rasputin?

Q: How did Rasputin die?

A: Boris Yeltsin, who was elected in June 1991.

A: The Romanovs. Descended from Michael Romanov, this dynasty included Peter the Great, Catherine the Great, and two Alexanders. Czar Nicholas II, the last Romanov ruler, was forced to abdicate in 1917.

A: Grigori Rasputin was a Siberian peasant farmer and faith healer who wielded great influence with the Imperial Russian ruling family. Alexis, the son and heir to the Russian throne, suffered from hemophilia, the bleeding disease, and the Tsarina believed that Rasputin could heal him.

A: On the night of December 16-17, 1916, three political opponents endeavored to kill Rasputin. First, they poisoned him, but it had no effect. Then, they shot him repeatedly, but, despite a torrent of bullets, Rasputin was still standing. Then, the would-be assassins threw the notorious Mad Monk into the Neva River, where he eventually drowned.

Q: What is the highest waterfall in the world?

Q: What is the highest waterfall in North America?

Q: How high is Niagara Falls?

Q: Where is the world's largest desert?

Q: What is the largest desert in North America?

A: Angel Falls, on the Carrao in Venezuela, at 3,212 feet.

A: Yosemite Falls, in California, with a total drop of 2,425 feet.

A: Canada's Horseshoe Falls are 158 feet high and 2,600 feet wide; the American Falls are 167 feet high and 1,000 feet wide.

A: The Sahara, in North Africa, encompasses 3,500,000 square miles.

A: Though tiny compared to the Sahara, the Chihuahuan gains that honor. Its 140,000 square miles include parts of Texas, Arizona, New Mexico, and the country of Mexico.

Q: What is the date of the first Wright Brothers airplane flight?

Q: When was the first Model T built?

Q: The Ryman Auditorium was well known as the home of what musical show? Where is it?

Q: What popular artist, who released a CD of heavy metal music in 1997, had a hit single in 1957 with a cover version of Little Richard's "Tutti Frutti"?

A: On December 17, 1903, Orville Wright piloted the first heavier-than-air, machine-powered flight in the history of the world. Although it lasted only twelve seconds, his 120-foot flight over the sandy dunes of Kitty Hawk, North Carolina, made him and his brother Wilbur immortal. A later flight that day went 852 feet.

A: Henry Ford first marketed the Model T in October 1908. Nicknamed the "Tin Lizzie," the car dominated American car sales for eighteen years.

A: *The Grand Ole Opry*, which has been a radio program for 75 years, moved to the Ryman Auditorium in 1943, and stayed there until the new Opry House was built in Opryland in 1974. The Ryman Auditorium is on Fifth Avenue North in Nashville, Tennessee.

A: Pat Boone, who had a Top 40 hit with "Tutti Frutti," also released a heavy metal tribute album, *In a Metal Mood*, in 1997.

Q: Where was William Shakespeare born?

Q: In what year was the Globe Theater built?

Q: When was Christopher Marlowe born? How did he die?

Q: Which Elizabethan dramatist narrowly escaped the gallows for murder?

Q: What is the name of William Shakespeare's wife?

Q: What did Shakespeare famously bequeath to his wife?

A: In Stratford-upon-Avon, England. He died on April 23, 1616, exactly fifty-two years after his birth.

A: In 1599, the Globe Theater was constructed, utilizing timbers from another theater.

A: Marlowe was also born in 1564. He was killed in a tavern brawl on May 30, 1593.

A: In 1598, Ben Jonson was almost executed for killing a fellow actor in a duel. Although he was reprieved, he was branded on the thumb for the felony.

A: Anne Hathaway. In 1582, Shakespeare married this farmer's daughter. She was twenty-six; he was eighteen.

A: The only item Shakespeare specifically willed to his spouse was his "second best bed." Because the best bed in Elizabethan times was traditionally reserved for visitors, Shakespeare's bequest might have been a sign of endearment, rather than the slight it first seems. In any case, by law, Anne Hathaway received one-third of her husband's estate.

Q: Who fought in the Trojan Wars?

Q: What was the Trojan Horse?

Q: Who were the combatants in the Persian Wars?

Q: Which ancient city-states were the main adversaries in the Peloponnesian Wars?

A: A coalition of Greek principalities fought against Troy. This war was the subject of Homer's *Iliad*. It is believed that the wars took place in the 12th century B.C.E.

A: According to classical literature, Odysseus conceived the clever idea of smuggling Achaean troops concealed in a wooden horse into Troy to defeat the hostile Trojans. Contrary to popular opinion, the horse was not presented to the unsuspecting Trojans as a gift. It was simply left in the abandoned Archaean camp outside the city walls. The Trojans took the bait, and the city was conquered.

A: The Greeks fought against the Persians for more than forty years, from 521 B.C.E. to 479 B.C.E. Herodotus' *History* provides much of the surviving information on this war.

A: Sparta and Athens. The First Peloponnesian War lasted from 431 to 421 B.C.E.; the second ended in 404 B.C.E., with Athens surrendering to Sparta. After this defeat, Athens went into a decline.

Q: Match the U.S. cities and their nicknames.

Detroit	The Windy City
New York	Big D
New Orleans	The Motor City
Chicago	The Big Easy
Dallas	The Big Apple

Q: What was the first capital of the United States?

Q: Which city is further east—Key West, Florida, or Lima, Peru?

Q: In which city was the first electric traffic light installed?

A: Detroit = The Motor City
New York = The Big Apple
New Orleans = The Big Easy
Chicago = The Windy City
Dallas = Big D

A: Both New York City and Philadelphia have a claim to the honor. George Washington was inaugurated as the first President at New York's Federal Hall, and the first sessions of Congress under the Constitution were convened in that city. However, Philadelphia was considered the de facto capital at the time of the Declaration of Independence.

A: Lima, Peru, is four degrees east of Key West. In fact, most of South America is east of North America. Lima, Peru, at 77W longitude is east of Key West at 81W longitude.

A: Cleveland, Ohio. When Garrett Morgan installed his device on the corner of East Euclid and East 105th Street, no other city in the world had an electric traffic signal. Morgan, the son of a freed slave, can be credited also with another life-saving invention: the gas mask.

Q: How do frogs tell us that the air pressure is decreasing?

Q: Do ducks sleep with their eyes closed?

Q: How much gas do cows expel? (Why do cows seldom get invited to parties?)

Q: How far does a skunk spray?

Q: What are the names of the nephews of Donald Duck?

A: Frogs croak more often when air pressure drops. Low air pressure brings stormy weather.

A: Yes and no. Ducks in the center of a group sleep with their eyes shut, but quackers on the edges will spend the night with one eye open.

A: Every day, the average cow emits thirty-five cubic feet of methane gas. Conferences on global warming have seriously discussed this embarrassing problem.

A: Skunks can spray their foul-smelling liquid up to ten feet. However, this pungent aroma can drift downwind as far as a mile and a half.

A: Huey, Dewey, and Louie.

Q: When was Scrabble invented?

Q: What is the bestselling board game on earth, and who invented it?

Q: How old is chess?

Q: What two letters are not on the telephone dial?

A: Unemployed architect Alfred M. Butt invented the game in 1931, but he couldn't settle on a name. He called his diversion "Lexiko," "It," and "Criss Cross," but made few sales. He and his partner, James Brunot, didn't produce games to be sold until 1948.

A: Charles B. Darrow of Germantown, Pennsylvania, is generally credited with having invented the game of Monopoly in 1933.

A: The prehistory and early history of chess are matters of great dispute. However, Chaturanga, which developed in India in the sixth century, has a strong claim to be the earliest clear ancestor of chess. The game entered Europe around the tenth century.

A: "Q" and "Z."

Q: What famous Egyptian city was founded by
   Alexander the Great in 331 B.C.E.?

Q: In what country are the remains of Petra located?

Q: Who were the Vandals?

Q: Who were the original Young Turks?

A: After Alexander the Great conquered Egypt, he established Alexandria, naming the port city in his own honor.

A: Petra, which was founded by Nabataean Arabs, is located in present-day Jordan. Once an important trading center, the abandoned city was forgotten by the Western world for hundreds of years before being rediscovered in the early 19th century.

A: They were a Germanic tribe that conquered Spain and Gaul, and sacked Rome in the 5th century.

A: The Young Turks were a coalition of Turkish nationalists and other reformers who, in 1908, seized power and forced the Sultan to restore a constitution and introduce social reforms, secularization, and industrialization to the Ottoman Empire.

Q: What is unique about Pluto's orbit around our Sun?

Q: What is the highest mountain in South America?

Q: Which mountain is the highest point on the continent of Africa?

Q: What is the highest point in Australia?

Q: Which of the fifty United States has the lowest high point?

A: Two things. First, Pluto's transit is not a circular orbit, but an elongated ellipse that takes 248 years to complete. For that reason, Pluto, the ninth planet, was closer to the sun for the last twenty years than the eighth planet. Second, Pluto manifests an unusual tilt of 17 degrees to the plane in which the Earth and the other planets orbit.

A: Mount Aconcagua in the Argentine Andes is 22,834 feet above sea level.

A: Kilimanjaro in Tanzania ranks as the highest mountain in Africa. Hemingway's favorite climb is 19,340 feet up.

A: At 7,310 feet, puny by most standards, Mt. Kosciusko is nevertheless the highest mountain on the continent Down Under.

A: Florida. No point in the Sunshine State is higher than Britton Hill, which is a mere 345 feet above sea level.

Q: On what day did Washington cross the Delaware?

Q: Besides Paul Revere, who else warned the good people of Concord that the British were coming?

Q: Which American military leaders captured Fort Ticonderoga from the British in the American Revolution?

Q: How did Alexander Hamilton die?

A: On Christmas Day, 1776, General George Washington crossed the Delaware River. The following day, he surprised and defeated the Hessians at Trenton, New Jersey. The Patriots' pursuit of the German mercenaries might have been slowed by their discovery of a large cache of Hessian rum.

A: Henry Wadsworth Longfellow's poem made Paul Revere immortal, but William Dawes and Samuel Prescott also braved that midnight ride on April 18, 1775. Of the trio, Revere played the least heroic—captured by British patrols, he was held for some time before being released without his horse.

A: Americans Ethan Allen and Benedict Arnold surprised the British and captured Fort Ticonderoga on May 10, 1775.

A: On July 11, 1804, Vice President Aaron Burr shot former Secretary of the Treasury Alexander Hamilton in a duel in Weehawken, New Jersey. Hamilton died the next day.

Q: Where was Frank Sinatra born?

Q: What was the name of Sinatra's first group?

Q: What role won Sinatra his only Oscar for acting?

Q: How many times was Frank Sinatra married?

A: Francis Albert Sinatra was born in Hoboken, New Jersey on December 12, 1915. He died on May 15, 1998, in Los Angeles.

A: The Hoboken Four. The quartet won a contest on *Major Bowes' Amateur Hour* in 1935. Frank was the lead singer.

A: Sinatra picked up the 1953 Best Supporting Actor award for his portrayal of Maggio in *From Here to Eternity*.

A: Four times. He was married to Nancy Barbato from 1939 to 1951, Ava Gardner from 1951 to 1957, Mia Farrow from 1966 to 1968, and, finally, Barbara Blakely Marx from 1976 until his death in 1998.

Q: "This wallpaper is killing me" are said to have been the last words of which famous author?

Q: When *Leaves of Grass* was first published in 1855, whose name appeared on the title page?

Q: "April is the cruelest month" is the beginning of what major 1922 poem?

Q: Early in his career, Samuel Clemens took the nom de plume "Mark Twain." What does "mark twain" mean?

A: This was the last quip of the seemingly unflappable Oscar Wilde.

A: No one's. Walt Whitman's book might be the most important book in the history of American poetry, but its first edition was issued anonymously.

A: T.S. Eliot opened *The Waste Land* with those now famous words.

A: "Mark twain" is a riverboat term meaning two fathoms deep (which is twelve feet). Former steamboat pilot Clemens took the name, he said, because "it has a richness about it; it was always a pleasant sound for a pilot to hear on a dark night; it meant safe water."

Q: What kind of bird is a raptor?

Q: What is unique about the migration pattern of the Arctic tern?

Q: What is unique about the migration of the Monarch butterfly?

Q: What do birds dream about?

Q: Do all dogs bark?

A: Raptors are birds of prey, such as hawks and eagles.

A: The Arctic tern breeds in the southern sections of the
    Arctic, and winters along pack ice near Antarctica –
    11,000 miles away! The distance that it travels is greater
    than that of any other species of bird.

A: The Monarch butterfly migrates over 2,000 miles from its
    summer home in the northern U.S. and southern Canada
    to the mountains of central Mexico. The most fascinating
    part of this story is that the migrating butterflies have
    never before been to the southern winter grounds! The
    generation flying to the southern winter grounds was
    hatched in the summer grounds up north.

A: According to a 1998 University of Chicago study, birds
    dream about singing. In fact, while asleep, zebra finches
    rehearse songs. (When they awake, they warble more per-
    fectly.)

A: No. The Basenji from Central Africa yodels, chortles,
    growls, and snarls, but never barks.

Q: When did Europeans first discover Canada?

Q: When did Basque fishermen establish whaling stations in Canada?

Q: Match the Canadian provinces with their capital cities:

New Brunswick   Regina

Nova Scotia   Victoria

British Columbia   Halifax

Alberta   Fredericton

Saskatchewan   Edmonton

Q: What symbol appears on the Canadian flag?

A: The Norse (Vikings) landed on the coast of
    Newfoundland around 1000 A.D.

A: Artifacts have been found to indicate that Basque whalers
    were in Labrador in the 16th century. It is estimated that
    over 17,000 whales were killed and processed in Southern
    Labrador between 1545 and 1585.

A: New Brunswick = Fredericton
    Nova Scotia = Halifax
    British Columbia = Victoria
    Alberta = Edmonton
    Saskatchewan = Regina

A: A red maple leaf, with eleven points. Canada adopted a
    new flag on February 15, 1965, doing away with the old
    Union Jack flag.

Q: What is the largest state in the U.S.?

Q: Which state is the smallest?

Q: Match the states and their nicknames.

Pennsylvania	Show Me State
Idaho	Volunteer State
Wisconsin	Magnolia State
Mississippi	Keystone State
Missouri	Gem State
Tennessee	Badger State

Q: Four states have capital cities named after American presidents. Can you name them?

A: Alaska, which is 570,374 square miles.

A: Rhode Island, with 1,231 square miles.

A: Pennsylvania = The Keystone State
   Idaho = The Gem State
   Wisconsin = The Badger State
   Mississippi = The Magnolia State
   Missouri = The Show Me State
   Tennessee = The Volunteer State

A: The four states and their presidential capitals are as follows: Mississippi (Jackson), Missouri (Jefferson City), Nebraska (Lincoln), and Wisconsin (Madison). Of course, hundreds of other American towns and cities have been named after presidents.

Q: Two NFL quarterbacks passed for more than 50,000 yards in their careers. Can you name them and their teams?

Q: Which team won the infamous "Heidi Bowl"?

Q: Which National Hockey League team has won the most Stanley Cup championships?

Q: Who is the holder of most of the scoring records in the NHL?

A: Miami quarterback Dan Marino had 61,361 passing yards in his 1983-1999 career. John Elway, the Denver Broncos play caller from 1983-1998, passed for 51,475 total yards. Had Warren Moon not spent six years in the Canadian Football League, he would have amassed even more than his 49,117 NFL passing yards.

A: In November 1968, the Oakland Raiders beat the New York Jets, 43-32, by scoring two touchdowns in the last 75 seconds of the game. But television fans missed the last-minute heroics. In the game's closing moments, with the Jets ahead 32-29, NBC preempted the contest with the children's special *Heidi*. Needless to say, it was a great occasion for outcry.

A: The Montreal Canadiens, with 23 championships.

A: Wayne Gretzky, who played from 1979 to 1999, finished his career holding or sharing 61 NHL records, including the most goals scored in a season, and most goals scored in a career.

Q: Who was the inventor of the vacuum cleaner?

Q: Who invented blue jeans?

Q: Did Elisha Graves Otis invent the elevator?

Q: Who invented the computer mouse?

A: Ives W. McGaffey devised the first vacuum cleaner in 1869. He called his crank-operated machine The Whirlwind. In 1901, Englishman Hubert Cecil Booth invented a large, horse-drawn unit powered by a gasoline engine, with long hoses fed through the windows. J. Murray Spangler of Canton, Ohio, invented the first functioning portable electric vacuum cleaner in 1907. It was built by the Hoover Company of New Berlin, Ohio, who rolled out their first electric Model O in 1908.

A: Jacob Davis, a Nevada tailor, came up with the idea of placing metal rivets on the denim at the points of strain. In 1873, he and Levi Strauss patented the process.

A: No, hoists already existed. But, in 1853, Otis invented the elevator brake so that they wouldn't fall—obviously, a necessary improvement.

A: Among Douglas C. Engelbart's two dozen patents is one for a "X-Y Position for a Display System," which is a prototype for the mouse. Although the device was invented in 1968, Engelbart's brainchild was not popularized until Apple used it in 1984.

Q: How many bones are there in the human body?

Q: How many bones are in a foot?

Q: Do any mammals fly?

Q: How many quills does a porcupine have?

Q: How does a porcupine use its quills?

A: Adult humans have 206 bones. Surprisingly, babies have more bones than adults. As the child matures, bones fuse together.

A: Each foot has nineteen bones, fourteen of those in the toes alone. The same number of bones are in a hand.

A: Yes, bats fly. Other mammals are superlative leapers and gliders, but only bats can actually fly.

A: Our expert extractor assures us that the porcupine has 30,000 quills.

A: The good news is that porcupines do not hurl their quills; the bad news is that the needle-sharp quills stick into a victim when a porcupine brushes against him. Ordinarily, the quills lay flat.